Machine Learning for Malware Detection

Strategies, Models, and Applications

Taylor Royce

DEDICATION

To all of the researchers, innovators, and defenders who put in endless effort to safeguard the digital world, guaranteeing resilience and safety in a constantly changing environment. This book is dedicated to the visionaries and forward-thinking professionals who are influencing cybersecurity's future and continuously pushing technological limits to protect what really counts.

To all the teams working across disciplines to make the world a safer, more connected place, and to my mentors and colleagues, whose knowledge and insights have been crucial in forming my understanding of this profession. I hope your commitment keeps motivating and bringing about change.

And lastly, to the silent guardians who operate in the background to make sure that everyone can benefit from a safe and reliable digital environment, their efforts are invisible but no less important. You should read this book.

DISCLAIMER

This book's content is intended solely for general informative purposes. Although every attempt has been taken to guarantee the content's authenticity and completeness, the author and publisher make no explicit or implied guarantees or warranties about the information's suitability for any given purpose or its dependability. It is entirely at your own responsibility to rely on such information.

Research, industry best practices, and expert knowledge that was available at the time of publishing served as the foundation for the information offered here. However, certain material may become antiquated or prone to change because of how quickly cybersecurity, machine learning, and technology are developing. For the most recent guidance or practices, it is recommended to speak with experts and current resources.

Any mistakes, omissions, or consequences resulting from using this book including but not limited to monetary loss, damages, or security breaches are not the responsibility of the author or publisher. Based on the information presented, the reader is solely responsible for their own actions.

Readers are advised to consult with appropriate professionals in the legal, medical, and professional domains if needed, as this book does not provide such advice.

CONTENTS

ACKNOWLEDGMENTS

Without the assistance, inspiration, and contributions of numerous individuals who have shared in this journey, this book would not have been possible. I want to express my sincere gratitude to everyone who helped make this effort a reality.

I want to start by expressing my gratitude to my family for their constant understanding and support. Throughout the writing process, their endurance and faith in me have been a continual source of support and inspiration. Your support means more to my loved ones than words can say.

Additionally, I want to express my sincere gratitude to the professionals, scholars, and practitioners working in the domains of cybersecurity and machine learning. It has been an honor to use your insights as I have studied these intricate subjects, and your work continues to influence and inform mine.

I would especially like to thank my mentors and coworkers for their essential advice and comments throughout the writing of this book. Your knowledge has influenced the caliber and scope of this work. You have challenged my preconceptions, forced me to think critically, and assisted me in honing my concepts.

We sincerely thank the group of editors, proofreaders, and designers who have helped make this project a reality for their meticulous attention to detail and dedication to quality. I appreciate your painstaking efforts to provide the best possible final product.

Lastly, I would like to thank all of the readers for their interest in this work. I sincerely hope that the information provided will be a useful tool for you in your personal or professional endeavors and that it will assist you in navigating the intricate world of cybersecurity and machine learning.

I am incredibly appreciative that this book is the result of the combined efforts of numerous ideas, voices, and experiences.

CHAPTER 1

OVERVIEW OF MACHINE LEARNING AND MALWARE

1.1 Malware's Development: From Viruses to Advanced Persistent Threats (APTs).

Historical Overview and Taxonomy of Malware

Since the beginning of computing, malware, short for "malicious software," has posed a constant threat to computer systems. Significant improvements in intricacy, stealth, and damage potential have been made throughout its history. Early malware, like viruses, was comparatively easy to distribute over floppy disks or infected files. These viruses were mostly destructive in nature, frequently intended to erase files or interfere with a system's regular operation. Because users had to manually contact the contaminated media, the transmission was usually slow.

The intricacy of malware increased along with the interconnectedness of computing. Worms and Trojan horses started to appear in the 1990s and 2000s. Trojans might pose as trustworthy software and trick users into unintentionally installing harmful code, while worms could propagate independently across networks by taking advantage of flaws in systems and software.

Along with the emergence of ransomware, adware, and spyware in the 2000s, there was a noticeable trend toward malware that was intended to extort money from users or collect sensitive data in addition to causing disruption. Malware behavior and strategies are always changing in response to increased cybersecurity awareness and ongoing risk mitigation initiatives.

These dangers are now divided into many categories by malware taxonomy, which includes, among others, viruses, worms, Trojan horses, ransomware, spyware, and rootkits. Even more complex risks are present in the current malware scene, such as Advanced Persistent risks (APTs), which are focused, protracted attacks frequently planned by highly trained, well-funded organizations. With the ultimate purpose of espionage, data theft, or destruction, these assaults are made to infiltrate a victim's system and keep access to it for months or even years.

Notable Changes in Malware Sophistication and Behavior

Malware has developed over time from simple, disruptive tools to extremely complex, focused attacks. Malware behavior has changed significantly, including:

- Increased Stealth: Early viruses frequently made their existence known by causing damage or by displaying overt symptoms of infection. However, modern malware is more stealthy, avoiding detection with methods like encryption and rootkits.

- APTs and other contemporary malware frequently target certain organizations or persons, whereas early malware was frequently indiscriminate, aiming to infect as many devices as possible. These assaults are more purposeful and extensive because the goal is frequently espionage or data theft.

- Exploitation of Zero-Day Vulnerabilities As systems

become more secure, hackers are using zero-day vulnerabilities, which are flaws that have not yet been discovered and can remain undiscovered until they are patched and made public, to launch their attacks.

1.2 Conventional Methods for Malware Identification

Heuristic, Sandboxing, and Signature-Based Approaches

Malware threat detection and mitigation have traditionally mostly relied on conventional techniques, each of which has pros and cons.

- A database of known malware signatures or patterns is created, and files and processes are scanned against these patterns using the Signature-Based Detection technique. The malware is notified when a match is discovered. Signature-based detection works well against known threats, but it has trouble identifying unknown or novel malware strains that haven't been uploaded to the signature database yet.

- Heuristic Analysis: By examining the behavior or structure of previously unidentified malware, heuristic approaches seek out suspicious patterns that mimic known malicious activity. Compared to signature-based techniques, this technology can detect new threats faster, but it may overlook more complex, well-disguised malware or produce false positives.

- Sandboxing: This method entails running dubious files or processes in a sandbox, which is a controlled, isolated environment, in order to study their behavior without endangering the integrity of the system. The malware is identified as malicious if it tries to carry out destructive operations, such as altering the system or gaining access to private information. Sandboxing works well for finding new malware, but it uses a lot of processing power and could miss malware that can avoid detection by acting in ways that are time-based or environment-aware.

Disabilities and Restrictions

Traditional detection techniques are useful, but they have a number of drawbacks:

- Only recognized threats are detected by Signature-Based Detection; new or polymorphic malware that changes its appearance to avoid detection can get past it.

- Heuristic Analysis: May overlook extremely complex threats that imitate normal behavior or generate false positives, marking innocuous software as malicious.

- Because sophisticated malware may be built to detect and steer clear of sandbox environments, sandboxing is resource-intensive and not infallible.

Additionally, these techniques are unable to keep up with the malware landscape's constant evolution. The shortcomings of conventional strategies are brought to light by cybercriminals' increasingly complex tactics, underscoring the necessity for more flexible and dynamic strategies.

1.3 Machine Learning Foundations

Supervised, unsupervised, and reinforcement learning are the three categories of machine learning.

A possible way to overcome the drawbacks of conventional malware detection techniques is machine learning (ML). Instead of depending on preset rules, machine learning may learn patterns and behaviors from data, allowing it to adapt to new, invisible threats.

- Supervised Learning: This method uses labeled data to train the model, which means that both the input data (such file features or system activity) and the intended output (like malware or benign) are supplied. Using the patterns it has discovered, the model learns to categorize fresh data. Models are trained on datasets of known malware and legitimate files in this popular malware detection technique.

- Unsupervised Learning: In contrast to supervised learning, unsupervised learning uses data without outputs that have been labeled. In the data, the model finds clusters or patterns that might point to the existence of harmful behavior. Unsupervised learning can be especially helpful in spotting anomalies that differ from a system's typical behavior or in identifying new dangers.

- Reinforcement Learning: This method involves rewarding a model for making the right judgments and punishing it for making the wrong ones. Reinforcement learning, while still relatively new in the cybersecurity space, has the potential to continuously enhance malware detection by dynamically adjusting to changing threats.

Main Ideas: Classification, Model Training, and Feature Engineering

- Feature Engineering: In machine learning, features are the distinct, quantifiable attributes or traits of the data. These characteristics could include file size, access patterns, API calls, and more in the context of malware identification. Feature engineering is the process of choosing these features and converting them into a format that machine learning algorithms can use. Achieving high detection accuracy requires careful feature selection.

- Model Training: In order to teach the algorithm to generate predictions or classifications, a lot of labeled data must be fed into it. The model's success is largely dependent on the caliber and volume of the training data.

- Classification: The objective of malware detection is to categorize data as either benign or malignant. In order to determine if a certain file, process, or network activity is dangerous or safe, machine learning models are taught to perform binary classification.

1.4 The Confluence of Cybersecurity and Machine Learning

The Benefits of ML for Malware Detection

Machine learning is especially well-suited for malware

detection because it can:

- Adapt to New Threats: By analyzing data trends and adjusting to previously unseen behaviors, machine learning (ML) can detect emerging patterns, whereas traditional methods such as signature-based detection fail when faced with new malware.

- Handle Complex Data: Malware can exhibit subtle and complex behaviors that necessitate advanced analysis of vast amounts of data. ML algorithms are more efficient than conventional techniques at analyzing and correlating data from a variety of sources (such as file attributes and network traffic).

- Minimize False Positives: ML models, as opposed to heuristic approaches, are able to distinguish between benign and malicious behavior with greater accuracy by learning from large datasets.

First Achievements and Growing Interest

Promising outcomes have already been shown in early machine learning applications in cybersecurity, especially in detecting new malware variants and increasing detection accuracy. There are still issues, though, like the requirement for enormous volumes of labeled data and the difficulty in deciphering the "black-box" nature of some sophisticated machine learning models. Many businesses are implementing machine learning-based solutions as part of their cybersecurity strategy, and despite these obstacles, the increased interest in ML for malware detection keeps driving research and development in this field.

Machine learning technologies have the ability to completely transform malware detection as they develop further, offering stronger, more dynamic, and adaptable defenses against a growing array of cyberthreats

CHAPTER 2

Understanding Malware Behavior

2.1 Malware Static vs. Dynamic Analysis

A crucial component of detecting and eliminating cybersecurity threats is the analysis of malware activity. The two main categories of malware analysis are static analysis and dynamic analysis. Although each approach has advantages and disadvantages of its own, they both offer distinctive insights into how malware functions.

Disassembling Code, Examining Files, and Tracking Behavior (Static Analysis)

Static analysis is a technique for analyzing malware without actually running it. Security researchers can learn important details about the malware's operation and its goals by breaking down the code. The fundamental methods used in static analysis consist of:

13

- Code Disassembly: By converting machine code into human-readable assembly language, disassemblers or decompilers allow malware to be reverse-engineered. Researchers can determine the reasoning behind the malware's operations, including any payload distribution systems, obfuscation techniques, or system interactions, by examining this code.

- File Inspection: Static file analysis entails looking at a suspicious file's content and structure. This could entail looking through the metadata of the file, deciphering code strings that are encoded in the file, or figuring out which encryption algorithms are being utilized to conceal data. Before the file is ever run, this kind of examination frequently reveals hidden features or harmful payloads that have been embedded.

In static analysis, researchers may also seek for any references or signs that might indicate the behavior of the malware after it has been executed. This is known as behavior tracing. These could involve network activities, file manipulations, or system calls.

Dynamic Analysis Behavior Tracing

In dynamic analysis, the virus is run in a controlled setting, typically a sandbox, to watch how it behaves in real time. Dynamic analysis, as opposed to static analysis, enables researchers to track how the virus interacts with files, the operating system, and network resources. The main benefit here is that researchers may observe directly how the malware functions, including:

- File System Changes: Researchers can see how the file system is changed by running the malware. This covers the creation of new files, modifications to existing files, and changes to file attributes.

- Network Communication: Researchers can also use dynamic analysis to see if the malware tries to connect to external servers, which can expose its command and control architecture or attempts at exfiltration.

Both static and dynamic analyses are crucial for developing a thorough understanding of malware because they offer distinct viewpoints. Static analysis reveals dangerous code and logic that has been embedded, while dynamic analysis demonstrates how the code acts in the real world.

2.2 Methods for Avoiding Malware

In order to avoid detection by both conventional security tools and contemporary analytic techniques, malware developers are increasingly using complex approaches. Recognizing these evasion strategies and creating remedies are essential to comprehending and reducing these risks.

Metamorphism, Polymorphism, and Code Obfuscation

- Code obfuscation is one of the main ways malware avoids detection. Obfuscation is the intentional modification of a malware file's code to make it harder to decipher without affecting its operation. Avoiding signature-based detection techniques that depend on well-known patterns is the goal. Obfuscation may consist of:

- Renaming Variables and Functions: Obfuscation makes code more difficult to understand and decipher by giving variables, functions, or system calls arbitrary or nonsensical names.

- Code Encryption: To stop static analysis tools from reading the malware's code, the creators of the malware can encrypt some parts of it. The malware encrypts itself in memory after it has been run, making it more difficult to examine without running the file.

- Polymorphism: Malware that is polymorphic alters its code every time it is run. This enables it to avoid detection systems that rely on known patterns and are based on signatures. The malware's appearance is changed, making it practically impossible for conventional security technologies to identify it, even though its fundamental operation stays the same.

- Metamorphism: By entirely rebuilding its code each time it runs, metamorphic malware goes beyond polymorphism without necessarily altering its functionality. Because no two instances of the infection are alike, even if they carry out the identical duties, detection becomes very challenging.

Anti-VM and Anti-Debugging Techniques

Malware frequently uses anti-debugging and anti-virtual machine (VM) tactics to thwart investigation. These strategies are intended to make it challenging for researchers to examine the malware in a secure setting. Typical methods include:

- Anti-Debugging: Malware is able to identify whether virtual environments or debugging tools are present. If it recognizes that it is being examined, it may purposefully crash, change its behavior, or turn off specific features, which would annoy reverse engineers who attempt to examine it.

- Anti-VM Strategies: Malware can be securely executed and observed in virtual environments (VMs) without endangering physical systems. Malware writers can identify when they are operating in a virtual machine (VM) using a variety of techniques. This can involve looking for indicators of virtualization (such particular hardware setups or VM-specific programs) and then changing its behavior or refusing to run in that environment.

These evasion strategies serve as a reminder that in order to keep ahead of increasingly complex threats, cybersecurity experts need to be alert and flexible, continuously improving their detection approaches.

2.3 Malicious Activity Behavioral Indicators

Malware can be found via behavioral analysis, particularly in situations where more conventional detection techniques are ineffective. Even if the malware's code is obfuscated or polymorphic, researchers can frequently detect malicious activities by looking at how a piece of software acts within a system.

File System Modifications, Registry Edits, and API Call Patterns

Malware frequently behaves differently from normal user behavior when interacting with the operating system and files. The following are important behavioral markers of malevolent activity:

- API Call Patterns: In order to carry out nefarious tasks like transmitting network traffic or deleting or creating files, malware frequently performs odd or suspicious API calls. Researchers can identify activity that deviates from the norm and indicates that malicious activity is occurring by monitoring these calls.

- File System Changes: Malware may change the file system by adding new files, editing already-existing files, or adjusting permissions. Changes that seem suspicious could be signs of infection, particularly if they occur suddenly or without user consent.

- Registry Edits: Malware frequently changes the registry on Windows computers in order to stay persistent or change how the system behaves. These adjustments could involve adding entries to starting pathways, turning off security software, or setting up services that are hidden and run continuously. A trustworthy sign of harmful activity is registry modifications.

Cybersecurity experts can monitor criminal activity by concentrating on these behavioral signs, even in cases where the underlying virus has been expressly created to evade detection using conventional techniques.

2.4 Behavior Profiling Difficulties

Behavior profiling has drawbacks even if it offers priceless insights into malware detection. Dealing with intricate, extremely sophisticated malware that is made to elude conventional analysis techniques is one of the main challenges.

Managing Packed Executables and Encrypted Payloads

To evade detection, many contemporary malware versions use packed executables or encrypted payloads. These methods further complicate the analyzing process:

- Encrypted Payloads: In order to conceal the actual nature of its harmful code, malware frequently encrypts its payloads. Static analysis finds it challenging to identify this encrypted payload because it is only decoded during runtime. Since the payload is only made visible when the malware runs, dynamic analysis may be the only method to see how the malware behaves in these situations.

- The process of compressing or encrypting executable code in order to mask its contents is known as "packing." Packing does not stop the malware from running, but it can make analysis more challenging. During dynamic analysis, unpacking techniques are frequently used to expose the file's underlying nature.

Because of these difficulties, cybersecurity experts must

continuously modify their approaches, combining static and dynamic analysis with specialized tools to decode the encrypted or obfuscated parts of contemporary malware.

Creating efficient detection and mitigation techniques requires an understanding of malware behavior. Cybersecurity professionals can greatly enhance their ability to fight malware by becoming proficient in both static and dynamic analysis approaches, identifying typical evasion tactics, and learning to recognize important behavioral indications. Even while there are still difficulties, the continuous improvement of analysis techniques keeps giving us the means to defend systems against ever-more-advanced attacks

CHAPTER 3

INFORMATION AS THE BASIS FOR IDENTIFICATION

The fight against malware in the field of cybersecurity is a continuous and dynamic conflict. But data is one of the most potent weapons in a cybersecurity professional's toolbox. The quality and type of the datasets used to train contemporary malware detection systems are equally as important to their effectiveness as complex algorithms. Large, varied, and well-structured datasets are necessary for machine learning (ML) models—which are frequently used in malware detection—to recognize trends, distinguish between benign and malicious behavior, and spot emerging risks.

This chapter explores in detail the vital role that data plays in malware detection, including feature engineering, dataset preparation, and the significance of high-quality datasets. By the conclusion, you will comprehend how machine learning-driven malware detection systems work best when data is managed properly.

3.1 Quality Datasets Are Important

Having access to high-quality datasets that faithfully depict the actual environment of cyber threats is essential for efficient malware identification. Even the most sophisticated machine learning models will have trouble producing precise predictions in the absence of the proper data.

Synthetic versus Real-World Malware Datasets

- The following are real-world malware datasets: Training reliable detection models requires real-world datasets, such as those collected from real malware samples in the wild. Numerous malware strains with varying families, behaviors, and obfuscation strategies can be found in these datasets. Models are better able to generalize and identify a wider range of malware because of the richness of real-world datasets. However, privacy issues, regulatory restrictions, and the requirement for precise labeling of enormous volumes of data can make it difficult to get high-quality, labeled real-world datasets.

- Synthetic Data: Synthetic data can be used as a workaround when real-world datasets are unavailable or insufficient. Artificially created synthetic data is used to replicate the traits of actual malware. Synthetic data frequently lacks the diversity and complexity present in real threats, despite the fact that it might be helpful for enhancing training sets. Therefore, it is important to properly create synthetic data to guarantee that it accurately matches malware behavior in the actual world without introducing artificial patterns or too many biases.

Difficulties with Labeling and Data Inequality

- Labeling Challenges: Supervised learning methods require accurate labeling. This entails giving each sample in the dataset the appropriate "label" in the context of malware identification (e.g., benign, harmful, or a specific malware family). But classifying malware samples is a difficult, time-consuming process that calls for experience. Reverse engineering malware samples, examining their behavior, and drawing conclusions about their nature are common steps in the process. The detection system's efficacy can be significantly impacted by even a minor labeling error.

• Data Imbalance: Data imbalance is one of the main obstacles to producing high-quality malware datasets. Because harmful files are frequently far less common than benign ones, malicious samples are underrepresented in datasets. Machine learning models may become biased toward benign samples as a result of this imbalance, which reduces their sensitivity in identifying uncommon or novel malware strains. To solve this problem, methods including oversampling, undersampling, and the use of synthetic data creation (such as SMOTE) are used; nevertheless, they also present difficulties in maintaining the accuracy and balance of the model.

3.2 Malware Detection Using Feature Engineering

The process of choosing, altering, or producing new features (variables) from unprocessed data in order to improve machine learning model performance is known as feature engineering. Feature engineering is essential to malware detection because it transforms unprocessed malware data into inputs that a machine learning algorithm can use.

Derivation of Features from Logs, System Calls, and Binaries

- Binaries: Compilations of malicious software are known as malware binaries. The amount of instructions, the kinds of system calls made, the size of the binary, and the existence of any suspicious sequences or encrypted parts are just a few of the features that may be extracted by binary analysis. These binaries can have their features extracted using tools like disassemblers and decompilers, which can then be fed into machine learning models for categorization.

- System calls serve as a conduit between an application that is currently running and the operating system. Malware frequently engages in dubious interactions with the operating system, like establishing network connections, generating files, or altering system settings. Researchers can find patterns of behavior that point to malicious activities by keeping an eye on and retrieving system call traces while suspected malware is running. Features that aid in differentiating between malicious and benign software can be found in system calls.

- Logs: Log files, especially those produced by firewalls, antivirus programs, and intrusion detection systems, offer useful behavioral information that can be utilized to extract features. Patterns like odd network activity, odd file system modifications, or attempts to get around security measures can be found by examining logs. These characteristics can assist in locating malware that signature-based systems might miss.

Dynamic vs Static Feature Sets

- Static feature sets are extracted without running the malicious software. This could entail taking characteristics like file size, entropy (a measure of unpredictability), or the existence of questionable strings out of the malware binary itself. Static analysis is quicker since it doesn't involve running the virus, but it is less successful against malware that is polymorphic or metamorphic, that is, malware that alters its structure to evade detection.

- Dynamic Feature Sets: By running the malware in a controlled setting and watching how it behaves, dynamic features can be extracted. These could include registry modifications, network activity, files produced or altered, and system calls. Dynamic analysis is time-consuming and computationally costly, but it offers a more realistic view of virus activities. The most potent results, however, are obtained when static and dynamic features are combined since they enhance one another's ability to detect malicious activity.

3.3 Normalization and Preprocessing of Datasets

To make sure a dataset is clean, consistent, and appropriate for use in machine learning models, preprocessing is essential once it has been assembled and features have been retrieved. Normalization and preprocessing are crucial processes in getting the data ready for peak performance.

Managing Missing Values, Outliers, and Feature Scaling

Data points that considerably deviate from the rest of the dataset are known as outliers. Outliers in malware datasets may suggest abnormalities that warrant further investigation or they may represent uncommon but important malware types. Outliers can either skew model performance or offer insightful information, therefore it's critical to choose whether to include or exclude them.

- Missing Values: In real-world datasets, missing data

is a frequent problem that can arise for a number of reasons. Because of mistakes in data gathering or labeling, malware samples might not always contain full feature sets. Either specialized algorithms that can handle missing data natively or imputation approaches, which substitute a statistical value (mean, median, mode) for the missing value, can be used to manage missing values.

- Feature Scaling: The scale of the features affects a lot of machine learning methods, especially those that use distance-based metrics (such k-nearest neighbors). Bias in model training may result from features with varying ranges, such as file size or the quantity of system calls. All features contribute equally to the model's predictions thanks to feature scaling. z-score standardization and min-max normalization are common methods.

3.4 Evaluation Protocols and Benchmark Datasets

Benchmark datasets and evaluation methodologies are required to assess and contrast various malware detection systems. These offer standardized data and techniques that enable researchers to consistently evaluate the effectiveness of different machine learning models.

Well-known datasets (like VirusShare and EMBER) and their applications

- EMBER: One of the most popular malware datasets in the cybersecurity space is EMBER. It is classified as either benign or malicious and includes millions of feature vectors that were taken from Windows executable files. EMBER, which focuses on features taken from static analysis of binaries, has emerged as a standard for assessing machine learning models in the context of malware detection.

- VirusShare: VirusShare is a sizable collection of virus samples that are openly accessible. It offers a huge selection of real-world malware samples, both known and unidentified. VirusShare is frequently used for threat research, malware detection tool development, and model training.

Evaluation Procedures

- Using consistent evaluation protocols is crucial for evaluating malware detection systems. Typical performance indicators consist of:

- Accuracy: The proportion of benign and malicious samples that were successfully categorized.

- Precision and Recall: Recall quantifies the percentage of actual positives that were properly detected, whereas precision quantifies the percentage of true positives among all positive predictions.

- The F1 score provides a balanced evaluation statistic by taking the harmonic mean of precision and recall.

- Plotting the true positive rate against the false positive rate, the Receiver Operating Characteristic (ROC) curve enables researchers to evaluate how well their model differentiates between benign and harmful samples.

These assessment procedures are essential for comparing the efficacy of various models and guaranteeing that detection systems operate dependably in practical settings.

The foundation of malware detection is data. Effective machine learning-based detection systems require well-designed features, high-quality datasets, and appropriate data preparation. Cybersecurity experts can make sure that their models are strong, dependable, and able to recognize even the most advanced malware strains by comprehending the complexities of dataset preparation and review. Data-driven strategies for countering cyberthreats must also change as they do

CHAPTER 4

UTILIZING MACHINE LEARNING METHODS

Machine learning has completely changed how cybersecurity experts identify and address malware threats. Security systems can detect new and emerging threats in addition to established malware strains by utilizing sophisticated machine learning techniques. This chapter examines some of the most significant machine learning methods for malware detection, ranging from more complex strategies like neural networks and unsupervised learning to more traditional algorithms like Decision Trees and Support Vector Machines (SVM). Cybersecurity professionals can improve their malware detection skills and keep ahead of emerging threats by comprehending how these methods operate and how they are used in the real world.

4.1 Malware Detection Classification Algorithms

Many malware detection systems are based on classification algorithms, which categorize input data (such attributes taken from malware samples) into predetermined groups (like benign or malignant). These algorithms identify patterns that differentiate across several classes by learning from labeled datasets. Determining whether a particular file or process is dangerous or benign is the aim of malware detection, frequently based on its behavior or features.

Decision Trees

- **Overview:** Choice Trees are straightforward but effective models that use a structure like a tree to categorize data. A feature (like the quantity of system calls) is represented by each node, and a decision based on the value of that feature is represented by each branch. Recursively dividing the data into subsets that improve homogeneity is how the tree is constructed. The sample's class is finally determined by the model at the leaves.

- Decision trees are popular in settings where

explainability is essential since they are simple to understand and the decision-making process is clear. They are especially adaptable in malware identification since they perform well with both numerical and categorical data.

- Disadvantages: Decision trees might overfit, especially if the dataset is short and the tree is deep. Additionally, they have trouble capturing intricate feature interactions, which is frequently necessary for sophisticated virus detection.

SVMs, or support vector machines,

- Overview: SVM is a potent classification algorithm that determines the best hyperplane for classifying data. This usually entails using features to differentiate between harmful and benign samples in malware detection. SVM may identify more intricate decision boundaries by employing a kernel function to convert the input into a higher-dimensional space.

- Benefits: SVM works well in high-dimensional

domains and can manage situations in which there are more characteristics than samples. When working with sparse or complex datasets, it is especially helpful for malware identification.

- SVMs have the potential to be computationally costly, particularly when working with huge datasets. Furthermore, selecting the appropriate kernel function and adjusting hyperparameters might be difficult and necessitate thorough testing.

Unexpected Woods

- Overview: Random Forests are a group of Decision Trees that collaborate to produce forecasts that are more accurate. A random subset of the data and characteristics is used to train each tree, and the outputs of all the trees are combined to decide the final classification (often by a majority vote).

- Benefits: Random Forests are resistant to overfitting since the variance is decreased by combining several trees. They can also effectively manage big datasets and perform well with both organized and unstructured data.

- Random Forests are less interpretable than single decision trees, notwithstanding their propensity for accuracy. The intricacy of the model may make it more difficult to comprehend the logic underlying specific forecasts.

The use of logistic regression

- Overview: One statistical technique for binary classification is logistic regression. It uses a logistic function to describe the likelihood that a sample will fall into a specific class (benevolent or malevolent). In spite of its name, it is a linear classifier that can be applied to malware detection classification tasks.

- The simplicity, interpretability, and computational efficiency of logistic regression make it a viable option for real-time virus detection systems. It works especially well when there is a roughly linear relationship between the attributes and the target variable.

- Disadvantages: Complex, nonlinear correlations between features may be difficult for logistic regression to capture. Additionally, it makes the assumption that the features are unrelated to one another, which is frequently untrue in malware datasets from the real world.

4.2 Group Learning Methods

Several models are combined using ensemble learning techniques to produce a more robust and accurate prediction system. By combining the output of several classifiers, these methods take advantage of the "wisdom of the crowd" and lower the possibility of biases or mistakes in individual models. Ensemble learning can greatly increase the accuracy and resilience of malware detection.

Bagging and Boosting Techniques

The goal of the ensemble technique known as "boosting" is to enhance the performance of weak learners, or models that perform marginally better than random guessing. Boosting involves training models one after the other, with each new model trying to fix the mistakes of the ones that came before it. Because they efficiently lower bias and variance, well-known boosting algorithms like AdaBoost and Gradient Boosting Machines (GBM) are frequently employed in malware detection.

- Boosting is a potent malware detection strategy since it increases the accuracy of weak models. Additionally, it usually performs well in datasets that are unbalanced, meaning that there are much more benign samples than malicious ones.

- Boosting algorithms have the potential to overfit, particularly when the basis models are overly intricate. In order to avoid underfitting or overfitting, they also need hyperparameters to be carefully adjusted.

Another ensemble technique is Bagging, also known as Bootstrap Aggregating, in which several models are trained separately on various random subsets of the dataset, and the outcomes are averaged (in regression) or voted on (in classification). Random Forests is a popular bagging example.

- By training several models on various data subsets, bagging lowers variance and overfitting. When the basic models are prone to overfitting, it works very well.

- Disadvantages: When the underlying models are poor or underperforming, bagging usually works less well. Because several models must be trained, it can also be computationally costly.

Benefits and Drawbacks of Cybersecurity Applications

- Boosting and bagging have both demonstrated encouraging outcomes in cybersecurity applications, especially in malware detection. Higher prediction accuracy is achieved by their capacity to combine numerous models, particularly when working with complicated, noisy, and unbalanced data.

- Cons: Ensemble approaches might be prohibitively expensive to compute, particularly when real-time detection is needed. Furthermore, even if ensemble approaches increase accuracy, they may also make the model harder to understand, which is problematic in many cybersecurity scenarios where explainability is crucial.

4.3 Deep Learning and Neural Networks

Among the most sophisticated machine learning methods currently in use are neural networks and deep learning. These techniques are perfect for tasks like malware classification since they are very good at spotting intricate, high-dimensional patterns in data.

CNNs, or convolutional neural networks

- Overview: CNNs are a kind of deep learning model that are particularly good at processing structured data that resembles a grid, like pictures. CNNs can be used in malware detection to examine malware binaries in a manner akin to that of image processing. CNNs are able to recognize patterns that point to malicious activity and determine spatial links by transforming the binary data into a matrix format.

- CNNs are very good at identifying intricate, hierarchical patterns and features in data. They perform exceptionally well in scenarios involving unstructured or raw data, for example, where conventional machine learning models can falter.

- Disadvantages: In order to train efficiently, CNNs need a lot of data and processing power. Furthermore, they are frequently regarded as "black-box" models, which makes it challenging to understand how they make decisions.

RNNs, or recurrent neural networks

- Overview: RNNs are perfect for evaluating time-dependent processes, including virus behavior over time, because they are made to handle sequential data. RNNs can, for instance, examine system call sequences or the temporal evolution of network traffic in malware detection to find unusual patterns suggestive of harmful behavior.

- Advantages: RNNs can identify complicated malware that changes over time by identifying temporal patterns and long-term dependencies in data.

- Disadvantages: RNNs are less effective than other models in some circumstances because of their difficulty in training and susceptibility to problems like vanishing gradients.

Malware Classification Application

Because they can examine raw malware data (such system logs or binary files) and extract high-level traits that differentiate harmful from benign activity, CNNs and RNNs have both demonstrated significant promise in the field of malware classification. These networks have an edge over conventional signature-based techniques because, when correctly trained, they can automatically adapt to new kinds of malware.

4.4 Unsupervised Learning and Anomaly Detection

To find novel or unidentified malware variants, unsupervised learning approaches are frequently used in conjunction with supervised learning strategies like categorization. When labeled data is scarce or unavailable, these techniques are especially helpful.

Grouping together

- Overview: Similar data points are grouped together by clustering techniques like K-means and DBSCAN. Clustering can be used in malware detection to find collections of malware samples that share traits, even if the samples aren't labeled. This can assist in identifying malware strains or variations that were previously unknown.

- Benefits: Clustering can highlight anomalies and hidden patterns that labeled data might miss. It's especially helpful for identifying zero-day malware, which hasn't been discovered in the wild yet.

- Disadvantages: Clustering techniques frequently demand that the number of clusters be predetermined, which might make malware detection challenging. Furthermore, the features chosen for analysis have a significant impact on the outcomes.

Autoencoders and Isolation Forests

Instead of profiling typical data points, an anomaly detection system called an isolation forest isolates abnormalities, also known as outliers. This method can be used in malware detection to find outlier samples that show possible malware by drastically departing from typical behavior.

One kind of neural network used for unsupervised learning is called an autoencoder. They acquire the ability to compress and then rebuild data into a lower-dimensional representation. By assessing the reconstruction error, autoencoders can find anomalous patterns in malware detection. A malware sample is marked as suspicious if its reconstruction error is noticeably greater than that of benign data.

An essential weapon in the battle against malware is machine learning. Using a mix of deep learning methods, ensemble approaches, classification algorithms, and unsupervised learning, cybersecurity experts can improve their capacity to identify and eliminate malware threats. The methods for fighting malware must change along with the threat landscape. By being aware of these machine learning techniques, we can keep ahead of the game and make sure that detection systems continue to be efficient in spotting known and unexpected dangers

CHAPTER 5

MACHINE LEARNING-BASED REAL-TIME MALWARE DETECTION

The threats presented by malware are growing more complex, and the cybersecurity landscape is always changing. Machine learning (ML)-powered real-time malware detection is becoming a vital remedy as traditional signature-based detection techniques are unable to keep up with these rapidly changing threats. The architecture of systems that facilitate real-time malware detection, the difficulties in adjusting to emerging threats, the trade-offs between detection accuracy and system performance, and the combination of machine learning and Endpoint Detection and Response (EDR) tools are the main topics of this chapter's exploration of machine learning's potential for malware detection.

5.1 Real-Time Detection System Architecture

A rigorous balancing act between data gathering, processing, and model deployment is necessary to design an effective real-time virus detection system. The form of the data pipeline and the way machine learning models are incorporated into the overall architecture are crucial to the detection system's efficient operation.

Design of Data Pipelines

- Data Collection: Collecting pertinent data for analysis is the initial stage in the data pipeline. This involves keeping an eye on system calls, file operations, network traffic, and user behavior in a real-time virus detection system. Depending on whether endpoint security, network security, or cloud infrastructure is the main focus, the data sources may differ. Here, the difficulty lies in making sure that data collecting doesn't overload the system with extraneous information or impair system performance.

- After the data is gathered, it needs to be preprocessed in order to be analyzed. Cleaning the data, dealing with missing values, normalizing values, and converting raw data into formats that machine learning models can use are all part of this process. This is an important step since the accuracy of the models used to detect malware is directly impacted by the quality of the input data.

- Feature Engineering: Feature engineering is the process of choosing and developing features that aid in spotting patterns suggestive of malicious activity in the context of malware detection. Metrics like the kinds of files accessed, the frequency of system calls, or the behavior of network connections may fall under this category. Designing useful features frequently requires domain understanding of malware characteristics.

- Model Deployment: Machine learning models must be deployed when the data pipeline is configured and features are prepared. How often the models are updated is a crucial factor. Because of the nature of real-time detection, the system needs to be able to deploy models rapidly without sacrificing accuracy.

This frequently calls for strong infrastructure that enables models to be deployed and retrained on a regular basis using fresh data without impairing system performance.

Complementing Real-Time Systems

Effective virus detection must be made possible by real-time solutions that cause the least amount of disturbance to the user experience. The machine learning model might be used, for example, as a component of the network traffic monitoring stack or as a kernel driver in an endpoint security system. The ultimate objective is seamless detection and prevention without observable delays or system slowdowns; however, the integration points will vary depending on the architecture of the system being secured.

5.2 Models of Online Learning

The ongoing evolution of malware is one of the biggest obstacles to real-time malware detection. The machine learning models that were successful yesterday could not be so today as new threats emerge and attackers hone their tactics. This problem can be effectively solved by online learning, which allows models to continuously learn and adjust to new data without requiring retraining from the beginning.

Continuous Learning to Adjust to Changing Malware

The definition of online learning A class of machine learning models that gradually update when fresh data becomes available is referred to as online learning. Online learning enables the model to learn constantly from a stream of incoming data, in contrast to batch learning, which retrains the model on a fixed dataset on a regular basis. Because it allows the model to adjust to changing malware behaviors without requiring whole retraining, this is perfect for malware detection.

- Advantages of Malware Detection: Malware frequently uses strategies like polymorphism and metamorphism to avoid detection, especially new and advanced varieties. Models can quickly adjust to these changes by integrating fresh information on malicious activity as it emerges thanks to online learning. To better identify new variations of a malware family, for instance, a model may use updated features to discover new malicious behavior patterns.

- Real-Time System Implementation: Real-time input of incoming data into the model is a feasible way to execute online learning. The model's comprehension is updated with each new data sample, such as a network packet or system call. In addition to making sure that updates are done in a method that preserves the model's accuracy and stability over time, the system must be built to manage this steady stream of data without experiencing performance degradation.

Difficulties with Online Education

- Ensuring that the incoming data is reflective of the entire danger landscape is a difficulty for online learning in malware detection. The model may fail to learn significant patterns or adapt inappropriately if the data stream is biased or contains noise. Careful observation and verification of the incoming data are necessary for this.

- Concept Drift: When the fundamental patterns in the data shift over time, this is known as concept drift. This could show up in malware detection as a change in the strategies or methods that malware developers employ. Although online learning models can adjust to some extent, they must be regularly observed to see whether idea drift is occurring and whether the model's functionality is declining.

5.3 Resource Limitations and Model Latency

A real-time system must strike a compromise between accuracy and speed. In order to prevent harmful behavior from spreading, malware detection must happen fast. At the same time, the process must remain highly accurate in order to reduce false positives and false negatives.

Keeping Accuracy, Speed, and System Overhead in Check

- Considerations of Latency: The term "latency" in real-time malware detection describes how long it takes the system to process, examine, and determine whether incoming data is harmful or benign. In settings like endpoint security, where a delayed response could allow malware to run and inflict harm, this latency must be kept to a minimum to prevent delays in system response.

- Model Complexity vs. Speed: The complexity of machine learning models can vary greatly. For instance, deep learning models are strong and can identify minute patterns in data, but they frequently have higher processing costs and take longer to infer. While simpler models, such as logistic regression or decision trees, are quicker, they might not be as good at identifying sophisticated threats. When creating a real-time malware detection system, striking the correct balance is crucial.

- Resource Constraints: CPU, memory, and storage are just a few of the resource limitations that real-time systems frequently face. The resource-intensive nature of deep learning models and intricate ensemble techniques may restrict their use in settings with limited resources. Updating models for resource efficiency without compromising speed is crucial to keeping a malware detection system that is both scalable and responsive.

Optimization Techniques

- Model Pruning: Model pruning is a technique for lowering the computational overhead of complex models. It entails eliminating model components that have no bearing on the final forecast. This can speed up inference and reduce the size of the model without significantly sacrificing accuracy.

- Edge Computing: Offloading a portion of the processing to edge devices or specialist hardware, such as GPUs or TPUs, may be advantageous in some situations. By processing data closer to the source, like at the endpoint or network gateway, this can help spread the computational load and lower latency.

- Model Quantization: Model quantization is another method to minimize the resource footprint. It entails lowering the precision of the model's weights, which lowers the amount of memory and processing needed for inference.

5.4 Combining Endpoint Detection and Response (EDR) Tools with Machine Learning

Machine learning can significantly increase the efficacy of EDR technologies, which are intended to monitor and address security risks at the endpoint level. By examining a variety of endpoint behaviors and activities, machine learning helps EDR systems identify known and novel malware.

Real-World Application and Use Cases

- Detection of Zero-Day Attacks: Detecting zero-day attacks is one of the main applications for ML-powered EDR tools. These attacks take use of flaws that haven't been found or fixed yet. Machine learning may examine patterns of activity and highlight abnormalities that can point to the existence of a zero-day attack, but traditional signature-based detection techniques are useless against such threats.

- Behavioral Analysis: By keeping an eye on the activities of the processes and applications that are operating on the endpoint, EDR systems that include machine learning can carry out behavioral analysis. The EDR system can identify any departures from the norm as possibly dangerous by knowing how programs typically behave. For instance, the EDR system may sound an alarm if an application that was previously innocuous starts altering important system files.

- Automated Response: Automated response systems can also be coupled with machine learning. The system can immediately isolate the compromised endpoint, stop malicious network activity, or even reverse system modifications to a previous state after detecting a possible malware threat. This prompt action can lessen damage and stop malware from spreading.

Difficulties with Integration

- Concerns around data privacy and compliance are brought up by integrating machine learning with EDR techniques, particularly when handling private or sensitive data. To make sure it conforms with laws like GDPR or HIPAA, the data gathered for malware detection needs to be treated carefully.

- False Positives: Handling false positives is one of the most difficult aspects of combining ML with EDR technologies. False positives have the potential to cause disturbances in a real-time setting by mistakenly classifying innocent programs as malicious. To reduce these false alerts, the models must be continuously adjusted.

Machine learning-powered real-time malware detection is a major advancement in the battle against online dangers.

Organizations can enhance their capacity to identify and stop attacks in real time by utilizing cutting-edge strategies including online learning, low-latency processing optimization, and endpoint detection system integration. These systems do have drawbacks, too, such as managing system resources, battling malware that is always changing, and striking a balance between speed and accuracy. Machine learning will become more and more important as the threat landscape changes to make sure cybersecurity protections can stay up

CHAPTER 6

ASSESSING AND ENHANCING MODEL EFFECTIVENESS

As machine learning (ML) models are used more and more to combat malware, it is crucial to assess their effectiveness to make sure they work well in actual cybersecurity settings. Because malware detection models must reliably differentiate between benign and harmful actions while functioning at scale and in real-time, they present specific difficulties. With an emphasis on performance measures, validation methods, handling errors such as false positives and false negatives, and improving model interpretability, this chapter explores the fundamentals of assessing and upgrading model performance.

6.1 Malware Detection Performance Metrics

Measuring a malware detection model's overall accuracy is only one aspect of assessing its performance. A more sophisticated set of criteria is needed to make sure the model can accurately identify malware without producing an excessive number of false alarms due to the dynamic and frequently hostile character of malware. Accuracy, precision, recall, F1-score, and ROC-AUC are important performance indicators. Let's take a closer look at these parameters and how they relate to malware detection.

Precision

The simplest performance statistic is accuracy, which is defined as the proportion of accurate forecasts (including true positives and true negatives) to all predictions. Although accuracy may provide a general idea of a model's effectiveness, it can be deceptive, particularly in datasets that are unbalanced and contain many more benign than malicious cases.

- Limitations: Because benign data is so common, a model that identifies the majority of samples as benign may nonetheless achieve high accuracy in malware identification. Nevertheless, such a model would not be able to efficiently detect malevolent conduct.

Accuracy

Precision is defined as the percentage of true positive predictions (malware that is successfully recognized) among all occurrences that are anticipated to be positive (including false positives and true positives). When the cost of false positives the incorrect classification of innocuous data as malicious is significant, it becomes even more crucial.

- Importance in Malware Detection: False positives can cause a lot of operational overhead in cybersecurity, including alert fatigue or banning legitimate applications. A model with a high precision score ensures smoother operations by producing fewer false-positive predictions.

Remember

- Definition: The percentage of true positives among all actual positive cases (i.e., the total number of malware samples) is called recall, sometimes referred to as sensitivity. This measure concentrates on the model's capacity to identify every potential piece of malware, which is essential for averting security lapses.

- Importance for Malware Identification: By ensuring that the model detects the majority of the malware present in the system, high recall helps to stop infestations from remaining unnoticed. Striking a balance is crucial since optimizing for recall alone may result in an increase in false positives.

F1-Score

The F1-score is defined as the harmonic mean of recall and precision. When both false positives and false negatives are serious issues, it offers a more impartial assessment metric. When a trade-off between recall and precision must be made, the F1-score is very helpful.

- The F1-score is important in malware detection since both false positives (stopping normal software) and false negatives (not detecting malware) can have serious repercussions. By keeping the two in check, the F1-score makes sure the model is neither very liberal nor overly constrictive.

ROC-AUC

The true positive rate, or recall, is shown against the false positive rate using the Receiver Operating Characteristic (ROC) curve. The model's overall performance is measured by the Area Under the Curve (AUC). A model that performs better is indicated by a higher AUC value.

- Importance in Malware Detection: ROC-AUC is especially helpful when comparing models or adjusting detection thresholds. It provides a general idea of how well the model can differentiate between harmful and benign actions under different operating circumstances.

6.2 Model Robustness and Cross-Validation

In cybersecurity, machine learning models must be reliable and accurate. By assessing the model's performance over several data subsets, cross-validation lowers the risk of overfitting and guarantees that the model performs effectively when applied to new data.

Overfitting Hazards

When a model learns to perform exceptionally well on training data but finds it difficult to generalize to new, unknown data, this is known as overfitting. This frequently occurs when the training data is not representative of the larger threat landscape or when a model is overly sophisticated.

- Impact on Malware Detection: Because cyberattacks are always changing, overfitting is especially troublesome in malware detection. An overfitting model might only be able to identify the particular malware types found in the training set, making it susceptible to novel variations or unidentified attack techniques.

Methods of Cross-Validation

The process of k-fold cross-validation involves dividing the dataset into k subsets, or "folds." The method is repeated k times, each time using a different fold as the test set. The model is trained on k-1 folds and tested on the remaining fold. By ensuring that all data points are used for both training and testing, this approach helps produce a more accurate indicator of model performance.

- Loo-CV (Leave-One-Out Cross-Validation): With this method, the remaining dataset is used for training, and each data point serves as a separate test set. Although LOO-CV might be computationally costly, it is particularly helpful when working with smaller datasets.

- Stratified Cross-Validation: This technique guarantees that each fold contains an equal number of positive and negative samples in situations when the dataset is unbalanced (i.e., more benign data than malicious data). In order to avoid the model being biased toward the majority class, this is crucial for virus identification.

Enhancing the Robustness of the Model

- Data augmentation, which creates fresh training data by transforming the existing data via transformations like rotation, scaling, or noise injection, is one technique to increase a model's robustness. As a result, the model has access to a wider variety of samples.

- Ensemble Methods: Ensemble learning, which involves training several models (such decision trees or random forests) and combining their predictions, is another tactic to increase resilience. By utilizing the advantages of many models, this lessens the chance of overfitting.

6.3 Dealing with False Positives and False Negatives

False positives and false negatives are two important error kinds in malware detection that can have a big effect on a system's usability and performance. Enhancing a malware detection system's overall efficacy requires an understanding of the real-world consequences of these mistakes.

False Positives

False positives happen when harmless data or actions are mistakenly categorized as harmful. This could lead to the quarantining of a crucial system file or the flagging of lawful software as malware in malware detection systems.

- Implications for Security in the Real World: Particularly in corporate settings where business-critical systems must run continuously, false positives can cause disruptions. Frequent false positives can occasionally cause alert fatigue, a condition in which security staff lose their sensitivity to the alerts and fail to recognize real threats.

- Minimizing False Positives: It's critical to concentrate on enhancing the model's accuracy and adjusting the detection thresholds in order to minimize false positives. The incidence of false positives can be reduced by using feature importance and modifying the model to better identify benign actions.

Erroneous Negative Results

Definition: When malware is mistakenly categorized as benign, false negatives happen. These mistakes are particularly risky in cybersecurity because they let harmful activity continue unnoticed, which could result in system penetration, data theft, or security breaches.

- Implications for Security in the Real World: In situations where preventing breaches is crucial, false negatives are crucial. If malware is not detected, attackers may be able to compromise systems and do serious harm before the threat is recognized.

- Reducing False Negatives: Using sophisticated methods like anomaly detection and improving the model's memory can assist lower false negatives. It's crucial to make sure the system is sensitive enough to identify questionable activity without sending out too many alarms.

6.4 Explainability and Interpretability of the Model

Interpreting and explaining the judgments made by machine learning models is essential as they get more complicated, especially in high-stakes fields like cybersecurity. Building trust, comprehending failure modes, and facilitating action based on model predictions all depend on the interpretability and explainability of the model.

Shapley Additive exPlanations, or SHAP,

- What is SHAP? SHAP is a technique that explains individual forecasts by determining how each attribute influences the outcome. Based on cooperative game theory, SHAP values offer a means of comprehending the effects of each feature on the model's output.

- Importance in Malware Detection: Cybersecurity experts can determine which characteristics are most suggestive of harmful activity by utilizing SHAP values. For instance, SHAP can assist in emphasizing the significance of a feature if a particular system call or network activity regularly results in malware detection.

Interpretable Local Model-agnostic Explanations, or LIME,

- What is LIME? LIME is an additional technique for elucidating machine learning model predictions. LIME concentrates on local explanations, which explains why the model made a certain decision for a single instance, as opposed to SHAP, which offers global reasons.

- The significance of LIME in malware detection is in its ability to help identify the reasons for the flagging of a specific file or action as malicious. Security teams can decide if an alert is a false positive or a real threat by using the localized explanation it provides.

Recognizing Decision Boundaries

Decision Boundaries:

- What Are They?: The thresholds or standards that the model uses to categorize data items are referred to as decision boundaries. Knowing the decision boundaries is essential for evaluating how well the model separates malicious from benign activity in the context of malware detection.

- Why This Is Important: Understanding the bounds of decision-making can assist pinpoint areas where the model may be erroneous (e.g., labeling innocuous behaviors as harmful). Data scientists and security specialists can enhance the model's functionality and modify its sensitivity by examining decision boundaries.

A crucial first step in guaranteeing the accuracy and resilience of malware detection systems is assessing and enhancing the performance of machine learning models. It is feasible to develop a system that functions well in actual security settings by utilizing the right performance measures, preventing overfitting with cross-validation methods, and resolving problems like false positives and false negatives. Furthermore, emphasizing model interpretability with techniques like SHAP and LIME can boost system confidence and offer useful information for raising detection accuracy. In the end, maintaining an advantage in the always changing field of cybersecurity threats requires efficient assessment and ongoing development of ML models

CHAPTER 7

CYBERSECURITY ADVERSARIAL MACHINE LEARNING

The necessity to comprehend cybersecurity's weaknesses against hostile attacks has increased as machine learning (ML) continues to transform the field. Techniques where attackers alter input data to trick or corrupt machine learning models are referred to as adversarial machine learning (AML). The complexities of adversarial attacks in the field of cybersecurity are examined in this chapter, along with their effects on malware detection systems, weaknesses that make models vulnerable to exploitation, and countermeasures. In order to prevent them from becoming the same things they are intended to protect against, it also addresses the ethical and security ramifications of applying ML models.

7.1 Overview of Adversarial Attacks

An emerging class of machine learning risks is known as

adversarial assaults, in which malevolent individuals purposefully alter input data to lead a model to produce inaccurate classifications or predictions. These attacks are especially dangerous in the field of cybersecurity since they have the potential to make vital systems inoperable, like malware detection models that incorrectly identify or categorize bad files. Evasion, poisoning, and model inversion assaults are the three main adversarial attack types that are pertinent to cybersecurity.

Evasion Attacks

Evasion attacks are defined as when an attacker quietly alters input data in order to avoid being detected by a machine learning model. In the case of malware detection, for instance, a malicious file may be changed so that, despite its continued impact, it no longer activates the model's detection system.

Evasion in malware detection could entail altering the infection's behavior or encrypting it in a way that renders the harmful code indistinguishable from harmless files. To get around security systems that depend on ML models, attackers may change particular features or conceal payloads.

- Example: "Backdoor attacks," in which a malicious payload is concealed inside an otherwise innocuous file, are a well-known type of evasion attack. The hidden threat is not detected by the model using its standard feature analysis.

Poisoning Incidents

In order to taint the machine learning model's learning process, poisoning attacks entail introducing malicious data into the training set. Attackers can affect the model's parameters by tampering with the training data, which can lead to the model misclassifying specific input types or performing poorly on real data that hasn't been seen.

- Real-World Impact: When it comes to malware detection, attackers can introduce phony, harmless files into the dataset that is used to train a model, which can distort the model's perception of what malware is. As a result, the system becomes weaker and more prone to mistake harmful files for benign ones.

- The trained model may learn to ignore particular features or behaviors typical of malware if an attacker inundated a training dataset with benign-looking files that contain minor malicious alterations. This would lower the system's overall capacity to identify genuine threats.

Attacks via Model Inversion

Model inversion attacks are defined as follows: sensitive or proprietary information about the model's training data is extracted by an attacker using access to the model's predictions. This could entail gathering information on the kind of malware the model has been trained on, which could aid attackers in creating more potent evasion tactics in the context of cybersecurity.

- Real-World Impact: If attackers are able to successfully reverse-engineer the model, they can modify their strategies to fit the model's flaws, producing malware that is even more harmful.

- Example: Based on the model's replies, attackers may determine the distribution of harmful and benign file attributes. Then, they could use the patterns they discovered to create malware that is particularly made to avoid detection.

7.2 Malware Detectors Based on Machine Learning Vulnerabilities

Although machine learning models have shown great potential in malware detection and mitigation, adversarial assaults can still affect them. These models are vulnerable to such exploits due to a number of fundamental flaws. Let's look at a few case studies of actual adversarial attacks and the flaws in malware detectors that they take use of.

Adversarial Malware Evasion in Antivirus Systems: Case Study No. 1

Evasion is the type of attack. The incident is as follows:

- Researchers employed adversarial machine learning

to create malware that may evade detection by avoiding signature-based systems in a noteworthy attack on conventional antivirus software. Without compromising its essential features, the malware was made to slightly change its behavior in order to avoid setting off the model's detection criteria.

- The model's primary weakness was its heavy reliance on static feature-based analysis (such as file hashes and byte patterns), which is susceptible to manipulation by adversaries. Furthermore, the model does not take into consideration the potential for new file variations or disguised code that might still be dangerous.

Case Study 2: Malware Detection System Poisoning Attacks

Type of Attack:

- Poisoning Event: In another instance, a malware detection system's training set was covertly altered by an attacker using poisoning techniques. The attacker tricked the model into misclassifying future malware samples as benign by inserting malicious files that were made to seem like benign ones.

- The model lacked tools to detect poisoned data points before their use in training, and the training process lacked protections against adversarial data. Moreover, the system was vulnerable to such manipulation since it lacked feature inspection and strong data validation.

Case Study 3: Cybersecurity Model Inversion Attacks

Attack Type:

- Inversion of the Model Incident: By examining the model's output and using that knowledge to recover private training data, researchers showed that model inversion attacks against malware detection models are feasible. This made it possible for attackers to create fresh malware variations that were suited to the model's particular flaws.

The primary weakness in this case was the absence of model transparency and inadequate security measures to stop unwanted access to model projections. Attackers could create more potent adversarial inputs by using the model's available outputs to understand its decision bounds.

7.3 Strong ML Models and Defensive Techniques

Strong defensive tactics are necessary to combat the growing threat of adversarial machine learning attacks. Machine learning models can be made more resilient to adversarial threats by utilizing a multifaceted strategy that incorporates ensemble hardening, input sanitization, and adversarial training.

Training for Adventure

Adversarial training is the process of adding adversarial samples to the training dataset. Small perturbations to the data that resemble the kinds of adversarial manipulations an attacker may use are used to create these examples. The model learns to recognize and fight against such attacks in the future by being exposed to these adversarial examples during training.

- Use in Malware Detection: Adversarial training for malware detection models would entail creating adversarial malware samples (modified files that still exhibit harmful behavior) and adding them to the training set. By doing this, the model is better able to identify minor changes without mistakenly identifying real dangers as harmless.

Sanitization of Input

Prior to feeding the input data into the machine learning model, input sanitization entails filtering or preprocessing it to eliminate any potentially hostile or harmful elements. This could entail employing methods to find and reject suspect data, such as noise filtering, anomaly detection, or heuristics.

- Application in Malware Detection: In the case of malware detection, input sanitization may entail employing static analysis techniques to flag files with odd or suspect behavior patterns before they are sent to the model for classification, or scanning files for known malicious signatures.

Hardening of the Ensemble

Definition: Ensemble approaches increase overall resilience by combining the predictions of several models. The possibility that an attacker may effectively fool a single model is decreased via ensemble hardening, which uses different model architectures or diverse hyperparameters.

- Use in Malware Identification: An ensemble of models, such as integrating support vector machines, decision trees, and neural networks, can be used in malware detection to guarantee that the other models will continue to produce accurate predictions even in the event that one is compromised by an adversarial assault. Because the attacker would have to take advantage of flaws in several models in order to succeed, this redundancy makes the system more resilient.

7.4 Implications for Ethics and Security

Machine learning models themselves are possible attack surfaces as they grow more and more important to cybersecurity. Because adversarial machine learning may unintentionally create new vulnerabilities, using these models in security systems raises ethical questions. Malicious actors may also take advantage of these flaws to interfere with operations or obtain illegal access. Despite being effective tools, it is crucial to make sure that machine learning models are not the focus of hostile exploitation.

Preventing ML Models from Developing into New Attack Surfaces

- Proactive Defense: Making sure that the application of machine learning does not unintentionally provide new weaknesses that attackers can take advantage of is one of the most urgent ethical issues. Security teams must constantly test and improve models to solve this issue and make sure they continue to withstand new threats.

- Ethical Data Use: The data used to train machine learning algorithms is also subject to ethical considerations. To avoid such breaches, sensitive data like user activity or private files must be handled carefully. Organizations should also think about the moral ramifications of developing systems that bad actors could use as weapons.

- Accountability and Transparency: When used in high-stakes cybersecurity systems, machine learning models should be open and honest about how they make decisions. This makes it possible for security teams to recognize model flaws and fix them appropriately. Measures for accountability should also be in place to guarantee that the choices made by ML models can be tracked down and examined.

In the realm of cybersecurity, adversarial machine learning is a new and important problem. We can better prepare for the weaknesses present in ML-based malware detection systems by learning about the several kinds of adversarial assaults, including evasion, poisoning, and model inversion, as well as by looking at real-world exploit case studies. Furthermore, the robustness of these models can be greatly increased by implementing defensive techniques like ensemble hardening, input sanitization, and adversarial training. In order to guarantee that machine learning models are safe, open, and impervious to abuse, ethical and security issues must also be given top focus. Resolving these issues will be essential to preserving a safe online environment as machine learning continues to play a major part in cybersecurity in the future

CHAPTER 8

FUTURE DIRECTIONS AND HYBRID METHODS

Machine learning (ML) has emerged as a potent instrument in the rapidly changing field of cybersecurity for identifying and thwarting threats like malware. But conventional detection methods, which have been used for many years, are still quite useful. In order to offer hybrid systems that integrate the best features of both machine learning and conventional detection techniques, this chapter examines their synergy. We also explore how malware detection will develop in the future, with an emphasis on context-aware systems, machine learning in threat intelligence, and combining edge and cloud computing to provide scalable, real-time security solutions.

8.1 Integrating Conventional Detection with ML

Using just one detection technique is frequently insufficient in the battle against constantly changing cyberthreats, especially malware. While traditional rule-based systems have the advantage of being highly interpretable and able to detect known risks with high accuracy, machine learning is excellent at recognizing complex, previously unforeseen hazards. Combining these two strategies will create hybrid systems that capitalize on the advantages of both machine learning and conventional techniques, which is where malware detection is headed.

Intelligent Models Added to Rule-Based Systems

Predefined rules that outline patterns of known malware behaviors or file signatures are the basis for the operation of traditional malware detection systems. These systems are quick and effective at spotting threats that have already been listed, but they are not very good at spotting novel or complex malware that hasn't been seen before.

- The ability of machine learning models to learn from data, recognize trends, and discover new dangers that might not be explicitly programmed into the rule base is known as Machine Learning Integration. Traditional systems' detection skills can be improved to handle unknown and changing threats by integrating machine learning (ML). To supplement the current rule-based approaches, machine learning algorithms, for example, can detect unusual activity or novel file signatures that do not match established patterns.

- Hybrid Systems in Action: The advantages of both systems can be combined with a hybrid approach. Rule-based models offer a fast and dependable initial line of defense by flagging recognized risks. Then, using sophisticated methods like classification, clustering, or anomaly detection, machine learning models can be utilized to evaluate any unfamiliar or suspicious files in order to find concealed malware. This two-pronged strategy increases detection capacity overall, decreases false positives, and increases accuracy.

ML-augmented antivirus software is one example.

Machine learning is being used more and more in conjunction with signature-based detection in modern antivirus applications. An antivirus program might, for instance, use ML algorithms to examine a file's behavior or characteristics that the signature database is unable to record after first scanning it with known virus signatures. As a result, a more thorough detection approach that can handle both known and unknown threats is produced.

8.2 Systems for Context-Aware Detection

By integrating environmental and user behavior aspects into the detection process, context-aware detection systems mark a substantial advancement in malware detection. These systems provide a more dynamic and nuanced approach to cybersecurity by adapting to the particular context in which a potential threat is recognized, rather than depending just on static data like file signatures or network traffic patterns.

Models Sensitive to the Environment

- Outlining the Situation: When determining whether an action or event is malicious, environment-sensitive models consider variables including the operating system, the user's position within an organization, the location, and the time of day. For example, if an attempt to access some important data takes place outside of regular business hours or is being carried out by a person who doesn't usually access those files, it may be reported as suspicious.

- By continuously learning from fresh data and modifying their criteria for what is considered typical behavior, these models are able to react to changing settings. For instance, the way a malware infection appears may vary according to whatever machine it is targeting. Detection systems can better identify hazards that could otherwise go undetected by taking the environmental context into account.

- Real-World Use Case: Context-aware detection may be essential in an enterprise setting. A context-aware system would identify potentially harmful conduct if an employee who normally deals with non-sensitive data suddenly started downloading a lot of classified information. Similarly, because of the unusual circumstances, an alarm would be raised if an employee in one area used resources that are typically only available in another.

Models Aware of User Behavior

- Behavioral Profiling: User-behavior-aware systems examine the normal patterns of behavior displayed by particular users in addition to the environmental context. This can include regular file accesses, login timings, browsing patterns, and more. Each user's typical behavior is established as a baseline, and the system may identify any variations from this pattern that could point to an insider threat or compromised account.

- Mechanisms of Adaptive Defense: The model continuously improves its comprehension of what defines typical activity as user behavior changes. This flexibility offers a continuous layer of defense against changing cyberthreats and guarantees that the system will continue to function well even as users' roles and behaviors change over time.

- As an Example in Action: Let's look at a sophisticated malware assault where a hacker obtains user credentials. Unusual behavior patterns, including reading files that aren't compatible with their regular workflow or signing in from an unknown IP address, would be detected by a user-behavior-aware system. To stop additional harm, this anomaly might set off a multi-layered security, like an automated alert or an account lock.

8.3 ML in Incident Response and Threat Intelligence

In addition to enhancing malware detection, machine learning is completely changing how businesses handle incident response and threat intelligence. Automation and intelligent systems are becoming essential for detecting, categorizing, and reacting to attacks in real time due to the increasing complexity and number of cyberthreats.

Classification of Automatic Threats

- AI-Driven Threat Intelligence: By examining

enormous volumes of data from several sources, including network traffic, endpoint logs, and external threat feeds, machine learning may be utilized to automatically classify and categorize threats. Security teams can swiftly recognize and address new risks without the need for human interaction thanks to this automated procedure.

- Real-World Application: In the event of a cyberattack, an ML system can identify the type of attack (e.g., ransomware, phishing, DDoS), classify the assault based on patterns from past attacks, and provide an instant evaluation of the threat's impact and severity. Instead of only responding to alarms without context, security teams may now prioritize responses based on the threat's characteristics and risk level.

Proactive Defense and Threat Hunting

- Using ML for Threat Hunting: By spotting trends that human analysts might overlook, machine learning can improve threat hunting. Through the use of advanced analytics, machine learning models are able to sort through large datasets in search of indications of breach or assault, such as anomalous network activity, altered files, or unsuccessful login attempts.

- Proactive Incident Response: ML models are also capable of foreseeing possible dangers before they develop into serious incidents. By continuously examining network traffic, for instance, machine learning (ML) systems are able to determine whether specific patterns are likely to lead to an attack, such data exfiltration, and initiate preventive actions, like limiting the traffic or isolating the attacked system.

Case Study: Detecting Ransomware with Machine Learning

Attacks using ransomware are notorious for their abrupt and destructive effects. Security systems can detect ransomware attacks before they fully spread by using machine learning to recognize anomalous file encryption patterns or the quick spread of encrypted files throughout a network. By taking prompt action, such as isolating compromised systems and stopping their spread, this proactive detection lessens the harm the assault causes.

8.4 Cloud-Based Malware Detection and Edge

Real-time malware detection now requires edge computing and cloud-based solutions as cybersecurity depends more and more on distributed systems. These technologies guarantee that security measures are not limited by network or hardware constraints by offering scalability, flexibility, and the capacity to react quickly to threats.

Architectures for Distributed Machine Learning

- Edge Computing for Local Detection: Edge computing enables malware analysis and detection to occur nearer to the data source, be it a networked endpoint or a user's device. By doing this, latency is decreased and danger detection and reaction times are accelerated. Edge systems can minimize the danger of malware spread by detecting suspicious activities in real time through local data processing.

- Cloud computing makes it possible to centralize security operations and provides the resources required to evaluate large amounts of data and respond to threats at scale. This allows for the scalability of cloud-based detection. Large volumes of data from dispersed devices and endpoints can be handled by cloud-based malware detection systems, which use machine learning algorithms to identify anomalies, categorize threats, and automatically activate defenses in several locations.

Quick Reaction and Flexibility

- Prompt Identification at the Periphery: Edge-based virus detection is especially helpful in settings like remote offices or Internet of Things (IoT) networks where low latency is essential. Even without cloud access, devices may continually monitor and analyze data locally by deploying machine learning models at the edge. This allows them to react to threats in milliseconds.

- Coordinated Defense Between Edge and Cloud: To ensure optimal efficacy, edge devices can transmit threat data in real-time to the cloud for long-term storage and additional analysis. To keep all network levels safe, the cloud may then compile this data, apply increasingly intricate models, and send changes back to the edge devices.

For instance, cloud malware detection and IoT

Thousands of devices in an IoT network might require constant malware monitoring. These devices can identify malware locally and prevent attacks from propagating throughout the network thanks to edge computing. Large-scale analytics and better long-term threat prediction are made possible by cloud-based systems' ability to compile threat data from various devices.

Hybrid techniques that combine machine learning with conventional systems are the way of the future for malware detection, improving the breadth and depth of threat detection. Context-aware systems respond to threats more dynamically and in real time by adjusting to the surroundings and user behavior. With automated threat classification and proactive defense tactics, machine learning's contribution to threat intelligence and incident response keeps developing. Lastly, scalable, distributed malware detection is provided via edge and cloud-based systems, guaranteeing that threats are identified and eliminated instantly, regardless of their source. These developments mark a new era in cybersecurity, when staying ahead of increasingly complex cyberthreats requires intelligence, flexibility, and scalability

CHAPTER 9

DIFFICULTIES, RESTRICTIONS, AND MORAL ISSUES

Machine learning (ML) is essential to improving threat identification and response in the quickly developing field of cybersecurity, especially in the fight against malware. However, there are difficulties and moral dilemmas associated with integrating machine learning into cybersecurity. This chapter explores the crucial topics of model openness, data privacy, legal compliance, malware detection biases, and the function of human expertise in machine learning-driven systems. Addressing these problems is crucial to ensuring that ML models are applied efficiently, fairly, and ethically as cybersecurity continues to rely more on AI.

9.1 Model Transparency and Data Privacy

Sensitive user data must frequently be gathered and analyzed in order to apply machine learning in cybersecurity. The capacity to acquire varied, high-quality data is essential for ML models to function effectively, yet this presents serious issues with data privacy and model transparency.

Managing User Information and Exclusive Malware Signatures

- Data Collection and Consent: The way user data is gathered, saved, and processed is one of the most important considerations when using ML models for malware detection. Large volumes of data, frequently containing sensitive or private information, are needed for ML models to be trained and improved. ML-based cybersecurity solutions must make sure that data collection practices respect user privacy. This entails getting users' explicit agreement before collecting their data, explaining how the data will be used, and making sure that sensitive data is anonymized whenever feasible.

- Data Minimization: Organizations should implement data minimization principles to reduce the risk of privacy violations and data breaches. This implies that only the information that is required should be gathered, used, and kept for as little time as feasible. For example, ML models could be trained on aggregated data that protects privacy while still yielding valuable insights, as opposed to constantly tracking every aspect of user activity.

- Organizations may rely on proprietary malware signatures, which are distinct identifiers for particular malware kinds that assist detection systems in flagging potentially dangerous files, when it comes to malware detection. Effective security and the requirement to safeguard intellectual property must be balanced in the development and application of these signatures. It's crucial to make sure that the signatures themselves don't unintentionally reveal private data, such user behavior patterns or system weaknesses, that could be used against you if malevolent actors manage to obtain it.

- Openness in Model Conduct: Gaining confidence in ML models used for malware detection requires transparency. Organizations and users must comprehend how these models work, what data they handle, and how choices are made. When it comes to cybersecurity, a "black-box" approach to machine learning where the inner workings of the model are opaque can be problematic, particularly when it comes to defending choices to end users or regulatory agencies. In order to overcome this, scientists are creating explainable AI (XAI) methods that seek to improve human interpretation of machine learning models without compromising efficiency.

Best Practices for Transparency and Privacy Protection

- Explainable AI (XAI): Using explainable models increases accountability by making it easier to understand the logic behind an ML system's decisions.

- Data Anonymization: To lower privacy threats, personal identifiers should be eliminated from the data sets.

- Encryption: An extra degree of security and privacy protection is added by making sure that all sensitive data is encrypted, both in transit and at rest.

9.2 The Regulatory and Legal Environment

The legal and regulatory environment around machine learning's application is becoming more and more significant as it is incorporated into cybersecurity. Frameworks that guarantee the ethical and responsible use of AI have started to be developed by governments and regulatory agencies, especially when sensitive data and automated decision-making are involved.

GDPR and Adherence

GDPR, or the General Data Protection Regulation: One of the most important pieces of law affecting the application of machine learning in cybersecurity is the GDPR, which governs the gathering and processing of personal data within the European Union. The GDPR's stringent regulations, which include requiring users' express agreement, granting them the right to data erasure, and providing them with an explanation for automated system decisions, must be followed by ML models that handle personal data.

- The GDPR's requirements for data minimization, user consent, and transparency must be adhered to by malware detection systems that process user data using machine learning algorithms. This could be problematic because malware detection frequently necessitates real-time data processing, which could involve examining user behavior or sensitive data. Finding a delicate balance between privacy compliance and efficient detection calls for careful planning and design.

- Cross-Border Data Flow: Data from several nations and jurisdictions is frequently needed by malware detection systems. It can be difficult to ensure adherence to international data protection regulations, particularly when moving data across borders. When implementing ML-based security systems abroad, organizations need to be mindful of local rules and regulations to prevent infractions and legal repercussions.

Automated Detection's Ethical Limitations

- Accountability in Decisions That Are Automated: The issue of responsibility becomes more significant as machine learning algorithms gain the ability to make judgments on their own. Who has responsibility if a system mistakenly marks a valid file as malicious? Who created the model the company implementing it, the users who supplied the data, or the developer? For automated technologies to be used ethically and in compliance with the law, clear lines of accountability must be established.

- Ethical Conundrums in Automation": Because ML-driven malware detection systems have the potential to rely too much on automation, they create ethical questions. Automation can expedite detection and reaction times, but it can also result in circumstances where human judgment's subtleties are missed. To guarantee that automated systems do not unintentionally cause harm, a balance between human monitoring and machine-driven judgments must be maintained.

9.3 Malware Detection Models: Bias and Fairness

Like any algorithms, machine learning models can produce unfair or erroneous predictions due to biases in the training data. Bias in malware detection can take several forms, ranging from disproportionately identifying files from particular user groups or geographical areas to favoring some malware kinds over others.

Unequal Representation Risks

- Dataset Bias: Historical events are frequently the basis of the data used to train machine learning models, which may not accurately reflect the range of contemporary cyberthreats. For instance, a malware detection system may be less successful at identifying malware that is more common in other locations if it is mostly trained on data from Western nations. Similarly, models that are less successful at identifying other kinds of attacks may be produced by datasets that over-represent particular malware types, such as those that target particular operating systems.

- Impact on Accuracy: Training data biases can have a major effect on malware detection algorithms' effectiveness. False positives (erroneously classifying benign files as dangerous) or false negatives (missed detections) might result from a model trained on biased data failing to identify new threats. This comprises the detecting system's dependability and credibility.

Resolving Prejudice in Malware Identification Models

- Diverse Data Sources: It is crucial to employ representative and diverse datasets that cover a broad range of threats, attack vectors, and geographical areas in order to minimize bias. Because of this diversity, the model is exposed to a wide range of malware behaviors and types, which improves its ability to detect threats in various scenarios.

- Fairness in the Design of Algorithms: Creating ML

models that are checked for bias and modified to make sure they don't disproportionately affect particular groups is the first step in creating fairness-aware algorithms. This could involve methods like applying fairness restrictions during model training, re-weighting specific data points, or modifying the classification criteria.

9.4 Human-in-the-Loop Systems, Adoption, and Trust

The issue of trust emerges as machine learning techniques are increasingly used in malware detection. Organizations and cybersecurity experts must trust that these systems are accurate, dependable, and able to make the right choices. However, human expertise is still crucial to the process because of the intricacy of ML models and the possibility of unexpected results.

Human Expertise's Function in ML-Powered Cybersecurity

- Systems that are Human-in-the-Loop (HITL): Even while ML models are capable of automatically identifying and categorizing threats, human specialists frequently produce the greatest results when they participate in the decision-making process. HITL systems integrate the advantages of machine learning and human intelligence, enabling cybersecurity experts' knowledge to inform the model's choices, particularly in circumstances that are unclear or complex. When a file is flagged as suspicious by an ML model, for instance, a human analyst may examine it to make sure it is not a false positive before proceeding.

- Establishing Credibility in ML Models: Over time, enterprises gain confidence in ML-driven cybersecurity systems, especially as they see how well they work in practical situations. However, the system needs to be dependable, transparent, and interpretable in order to build trust. Businesses should spend money on explainability tools and make sure that their machine learning models are updated and reviewed frequently to account for emerging risks.

- The Prospects for Human-Machine Cooperation: ML models will get better at processing massive amounts of data and identifying complex dangers as they develop further. Human monitoring will still be required, though, especially when there are important choices to be made or complicated ethical issues to address. The cooperation of machine learning models and human experts will determine the future of malware detection, resulting in a more potent and adaptable defense against online threats.

Unquestionably, machine learning has transformed cybersecurity in general and malware detection in particular. However, there are a number of difficulties and moral dilemmas associated with incorporating ML systems into security procedures that need to be resolved. The success and reliability of ML-based detection systems are largely dependent on a number of important issues, including bias, data privacy, openness, regulatory compliance, and the role of human oversight. In order to ensure that machine learning is a positive force in the always changing fight against cyber dangers, it is crucial that we maintain a balance between automation and human judgment as we continue to improve these technologies

CHAPTER 10

WHAT'S NEXT

The field of cybersecurity is going through a radical change. Machine learning (ML) is becoming more and more important in protecting against cyberattacks. But as these developments progress, they also present new difficulties, such as the possibility of malware that is much more advanced and the requirement for interdisciplinary cooperation. The future of machine learning in cybersecurity is examined in this chapter, with particular attention paid to predicted patterns, malware evolution, collaborative potential, and how businesses may create robust defense ecosystems to fend off future attacks.

10.1 Cybersecurity and Machine Learning Predictive Trends

Already, machine learning has shown itself to be a very useful weapon in the battle against online dangers. The next generation of ML-powered cybersecurity solutions is anticipated to be shaped by a number of significant themes. In addition to improving current systems, these trends aim to address new dangers in ways that were previously unthinkable.

Security Orchestration Driven by AI

The development of AI-powered security orchestration is one of the most important trends that will emerge in the future. This idea entails combining machine learning algorithms with other security tools to automatically identify, evaluate, and react to online threats instantly. These systems will automatically coordinate security efforts across several platforms, eliminating the need for human interaction to triage alarms or neutralize threats. This implies that the system can immediately isolate the impacted devices, fix vulnerabilities, and even put countermeasures in place to stop additional harm when a danger is identified, whether it be a malware infection, phishing attempt, or data breach.

- Predicting Future Attacks: AI's capacity to foresee

cyberattacks before they happen represents yet another significant advancement. By evaluating historical data, network traffic patterns, and threat actor behavior, AI systems can estimate when and where an attack is likely to happen. For example, predictive models could notice odd traffic surges or anomalies in system behavior, warning a potential assault. This proactive approach allows firms to reinforce defenses and prevent breaches before they grow into full-scale crises.

- Adaptive Security Systems: AI-driven security orchestration enables systems to adjust to emerging threats without the need for configuration modifications or human upgrades. ML models have the ability to continuously learn from fresh data and modify their reaction mechanisms as necessary. This flexibility will be essential in addressing the growing complexity and speed of cyberattacks, when security measures from the past might not be sufficient to fend off threats from the future.

Architecture of Zero-Trust

The importance of truthfulness The idea of zero-trust architecture, or ZTA, has been very popular recently and is expected to be a key component of cybersecurity frameworks in the future. Zero-trust security models presume that every person, device, and application inside or outside the network is potentially compromised, in contrast to traditional security models that rely on perimeter defenses (like firewalls) to defend the network. ZTA therefore mandates ongoing verification of all actions, regardless of their source.

- ML in Systems with Zero Trust: ML will be essential for assessing user behavior and network activity in real-time in a zero-trust setting. AI systems can assess if an entity's activities are consistent with predicted behavior by examining enormous volumes of data, including login locations, device health, and past behavior. The system has the ability to immediately initiate extra security checks or limit access until more verification is completed if anomalies are found. The risk of external attacks and insider threats can be considerably decreased with this degree of context-aware, real-time authentication and monitoring.

Therefore, identifying and addressing attacks is only one aspect of cybersecurity's future; another is anticipating and proactively managing risks via AI-powered orchestration and zero-trust models.

10.2 Malware's Development in the AI Age

Machine learning is changing how cybersecurity functions and is also having an impact on how malware evolves. The current difficult process of protecting against malware may become even more difficult as cybercriminals use AI and ML techniques to craft increasingly complex and elusive attacks.

Malware Produced by AI and Its Consequences

- Malware with Adversarial AI: The use of adversarial AI to produce malware that can learn and adjust to defenses is one of the most alarming trends in the field of cybercrime. By carefully altering the data used to train machine learning models, adversarial attacks cause them to incorrectly identify harmful activity as innocuous. This might make it possible for thieves to produce software that can evade detection systems, making typical cybersecurity solutions useless. AI-driven malware, for instance, may change its code or behavior in real time, making it nearly impossible for static detection techniques to identify it.

- Self-evolving malware, which uses artificial intelligence (AI) to adapt its behavior according to the environment it runs in, is another new threat. This kind of malware may adjust to various operating systems, security tools, or network configurations instead of depending on predetermined instructions, which makes it more challenging to identify and remove. Malware driven by AI may be able to recognize holes in certain systems and modify its strategy to take advantage of them, putting defenders and cybercriminals in a game of cat and mouse.

- Automated Phishing and Social Engineering: AI is also capable of producing incredibly realistic social engineering and phishing attacks. Machine learning models can create personalized messages that are very likely to trick people into divulging private information by examining enormous volumes of personal data from social media and other sources. Because these AI-powered attacks can imitate the writing style, tone, and substance of a genuine communication, it is increasingly difficult for consumers to distinguish between authentic and fraudulent emails or messages, making them more challenging to detect.

As a result of these developments, cybersecurity systems need to become more intelligent and flexible, use AI to identify, evaluate, and eliminate AI-driven risks before they have a chance to do serious harm.

10.3 Possibilities for Collaboration Across Disciplines

A single discipline won't be enough to shape cybersecurity's future. It will be essential for different fields to work together in order to stay up with the sophistication of contemporary threats. Each of these groups from data scientists and threat researchers to policymakers will be essential in designing the tactics and tools that will protect against upcoming cyberthreats.

Collaborating with Policymakers, Data Scientists, and Threat Researchers

- Experts in cybersecurity and threat research: Research is the primary line of defense against changing cyberthreats. To find new vulnerabilities, create detection models that are more precise, and comprehend the strategies employed by hackers, cooperation between ML developers and threat researchers will be crucial. To remain ahead of AI-driven malware and make sure defensive systems can keep up with the most recent developments in hostile AI technology, research will also be necessary.

- Machine learning engineers and data scientists: Building the datasets that drive machine learning models for cybersecurity will continue to be a critical function of data scientists. The caliber and variety of the data utilized to train these models determine their accuracy. To make sure that their models are as reliable and broadly applicable as possible without overfitting to certain threat categories, data scientists and machine learning engineers will need to work closely together. Building systems that can dynamically learn and adjust to new threats in real-time will also require cooperation between these specialists.

- Regulatory and Policymakers: Governments and regulatory agencies will need to develop new frameworks and policies in response to the growing complexity of cybersecurity threats, particularly those incorporating AI and machine learning. To make sure that legislation stay up with technological changes, cooperation between legislators, cybersecurity specialists, and technologists will be essential. Strong legal frameworks and international cooperation will be required to address issues like data privacy, the ethical application of AI, and cross-border cybercrime.

Organizations will be better prepared to foresee and combat the quickly changing dangers in the cybersecurity landscape by encouraging cooperation across these diverse groups.

10.4 Creating Robust Cyber Defense Environments

Future cybersecurity success depends on how companies develop their entire defensive ecosystems as much as on cutting-edge technologies. To guarantee the long-term security of digital infrastructures, a robust cybersecurity defense ecosystem combines proactive technology, responsive tactics, and close cooperation.

Strategic Advice for Governments and Businesses

- Purchasing Defense Systems Driven by AI: Organizations must invest in solutions that integrate machine learning, predictive analytics, and real-time threat intelligence as AI-powered tools become increasingly important in detecting and reducing threats. Implementing tools is only one aspect of it; another is combining them into a coherent system that can address a variety of cyberthreats in different domains.

- Encouraging Cybersecurity Education and Knowledge: The human element is a significant weakness in any security mechanism. Employees and users will always be the first line of defense, regardless of how sophisticated the technology is. To guarantee that staff members can recognize phishing efforts, adhere to appropriate security procedures, and comprehend the possible repercussions of breaches, it is important to set up ongoing training programs.

- Putting Incident Response Plans into Practice: Organizations must plan for the inevitable—cyber incidents will occur—in addition to taking preventive action. Organizations can react swiftly and efficiently to breaches when they have a clear incident response plan in place. These strategies ought to include human supervision, ML-driven detection systems, and explicit procedures for handling and lessening the consequences of a breach.

- Building Public-Private Partnerships: To build a more robust cybersecurity infrastructure, governments and businesses must collaborate. Partnerships between the public and private sectors can help with information exchange, collaborative research, and coordinated responses to cyberthreats. The overall cybersecurity posture can be considerably improved by pooling the resources and knowledge of both industries.

Resilient defense ecosystems are even more important as cyber attacks increase in complexity and scope. To withstand future attacks and offer long-lasting protection, organizations must create cybersecurity frameworks that are strong, flexible, and cooperative.

Cybersecurity's future will be shaped by ongoing innovation and cooperation. The techniques employed by cybercriminals will change in tandem with machine learning. Organizations must use cutting-edge technologies like real-time predictive systems, zero-trust models, and orchestration driven by AI in order to remain ahead of these challenges. However, creating practical solutions will require cooperation from data scientists, cybersecurity experts, legislators, and other stakeholders. Building robust defensive ecosystems and emphasizing interdisciplinary collaborations will help us develop a proactive, flexible cybersecurity environment that can handle the difficulties posed by tomorrow's cyberthreats.

ABOUT THE AUTHOR

 Author and thought leader in the IT field Taylor Royce is well known. He has a two-decade career and is an expert at tech trend analysis and forecasting, which enables a wide audience to understand complicated concepts.

Royce's considerable involvement in the IT industry stemmed from his passion with technology, which he developed during his computer science studies. He has extensive knowledge of the industry because of his experience in both software development and strategic consulting.

Known for his research and lucidity, he has written multiple best-selling books and contributed to esteemed tech periodicals. Translations of Royce's books throughout the world demonstrate his impact.

Royce is a well-known authority on emerging technologies

and their effects on society, frequently requested as a speaker at international conferences and as a guest on tech podcasts. He promotes the development of ethical technology, emphasizing problems like data privacy and the digital divide.

In addition, with a focus on sustainable industry growth, Royce mentors upcoming tech experts and supports IT education projects. Taylor Royce is well known for his ability to combine analytical thinking with technical know-how. He sees a time when technology will ethically benefit humanity.

www.ingramcontent.com/pod-product-compliance
Lightning Source LLC
La Vergne TN
LVHW022349060326
832902LV00022B/4341